HOW THEY LIVED

A VIKING SAILOR

CHRISTOPHER GIBB

Illustrated by
John James

ROURKE ENTERPRISES, INC.
Vero Beach, Florida 32964

First published in the
United States in 1987 by
Rourke Enterprises, Inc.
PO Box 3328, Vero Beach,
Florida 32964

First published in 1986 by
Wayland (Publishers) Limited
61 Western Road, Hove
East Sussex BN3 1JD, England

© Copyright 1986 Wayland (Publishers) Limited

Phototypeset by Kalligraphics Ltd, Redhill, Surrey
Printed in Italy by G. Canale & C.S.p.A., Turin

Library of Congress Cataloging-in-Publication Data

Gibb, Christopher.
A Viking sailor.

(How they lived)
Bibliography: p.
Includes index.
Summary: Describes the life of Vikings as sailors,
warriors, farmers, craftsmen, and traders. Also
discusses their homes, religion, customs, and family
life. Includes a glossary of terms.
1. Vikings—Juvenile literature. [1. Vikings]
I. James, John, 1959– ill. II. Title. III. Series:
How they lived (Vero Beach, Fla.)
DL65.G49   1987   948′.02   86–20265

ISBN 0–86592–141–5

CONTENTS

THE FURY OF THE NORTHMEN

A tall, fair-haired man drove his oar deep into the water. With him in the boat, forty other men grunted as they rowed. Swiftly, the slender ship sped toward the shore . . .

On a nearby clifftop, two farmers looked curiously at the beautiful ship. But their curiosity soon turned to horror. For as soon as the boat reached the beach, fierce warriors leapt from its sides, yelling and waving their swords. In a few hours the harbor and small town were burning ruins. When the beautiful ship at last sailed out to sea, there was nobody left alive to watch it go.

These fierce warriors were Vikings. They came from Scandinavia –

the countries we now call Denmark, Norway and Sweden in northern Europe. For over 300 years, between A.D. 789 and 1100, they set sail in their longships to raid and explore the world. They settled in Ireland and invaded England. They raided the Mediterranean, founded Normandy and traveled far into Russia. The bravest and most adventurous of them crossed the Atlantic Ocean to Iceland and Greenland. A few even reached North America – 500 years before Columbus.

The Vikings were not only sailors and warriors. They were also

The Vikings came from the lands we now call Scandinavia.

farmers, craftsmen, townsmen and traders. But they will be best remembered for their skill as sailors and for their beautiful ships.

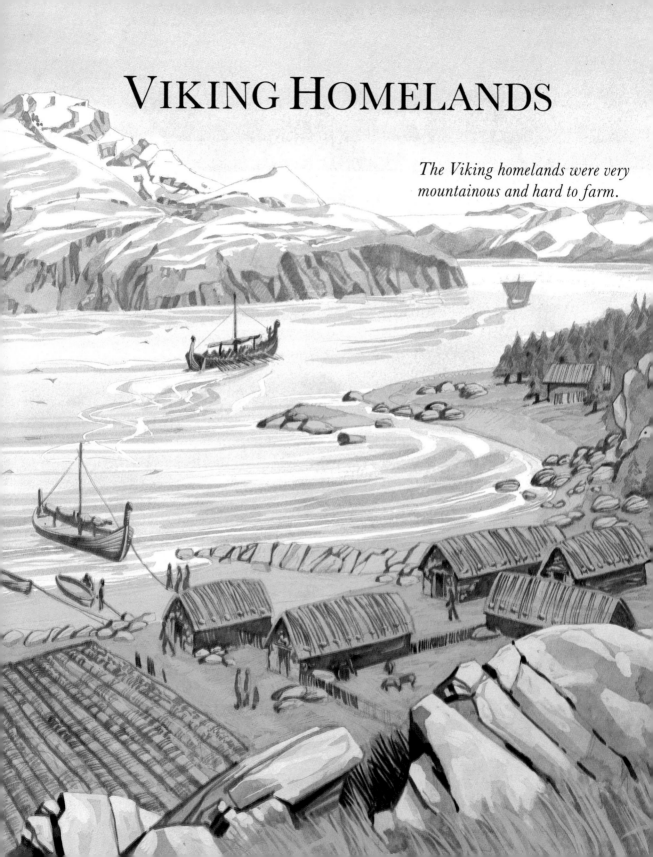

VIKING HOMELANDS

The Viking homelands were very mountainous and hard to farm.

The name "Viking" may come from an old Icelandic word "vic," which means a bay or inlet. Scandinavia is famous for its deep inlets, (fjords), and it was on the banks of these that many Vikings lived. There was also the expression to go "a-viking," meaning to go on an adventurous raid.

Viking society was divided into three main classes. At the top were chieftains, called *jarls*, who owned most of the land. In the middle came the free farmers, craftsmen and sailors, called *karls*. At the bottom of the heap was the *thrall*, or slave, who did all the undesirable jobs.

Why did the Viking sailors leave their homes to explore and travel the

This pail has been beautifully decorated by Viking craftsmen.

high seas? Many left for adventure and to plunder cities. But there were other more practical reasons, too. The cold climate and poor soil in Scandinavia meant that farming was very hard work. Often there were not enough farms to go around. If the population suddenly grew, many people had to leave their homes to search for new lands elsewhere. Some Vikings left because they did not like the way they were treated by their rulers; a few fled to escape punishment for serious crimes.

However, the Vikings would not have been successful if it had not been for one important thing. They perfected a new kind of ship which was better than any other in Europe. It was the "longship" that made the Viking Age possible.

Tenth-century iron tools from Gotland, in Sweden.

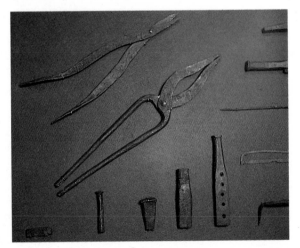

7

THE LONGSHIP

The Vikings loved their ships. They wrote songs and poems about them, and gave them names like *Wave Walker*, *Long Serpent* and *Raven of the Wind*. By A.D. 800 they had become the best shipbuilders in Europe.

Viking shipbuilders had no careful plans to help them. They relied upon the skill of their eye and hand. They used only simple tools – axes, saws and adzes. The ship's keel was the first thing to be laid down. Then rows of overlapping planks were nailed onto the keel and to each other. This planking was tied, or lashed, onto a

framework of ribs and crossbeams which rested on the keel.

The Viking longship had a very special design. It was usually made of oak and was long and narrow with a very shallow keel. This meant that the Vikings could sail far up rivers without running aground. They could also easily beach their boats on a sandy shore, or even drag them overland between two rivers.

The longship usually had a single sail, often brightly colored, and rows of oars down both sides. The bow and stern of the ship were carved with fierce animal or human heads. This was to keep away evil spirits, but also to terrify their enemies. When entering port or going into battle, the Vikings sometimes fixed their colorful shields along the sides of the ship. No wonder people fled when they saw the longships coming!

Viking craftsmen at work on a longship. The vessels were clinker-built, meaning they had overlapping planks. Some of the largest warships were up to 180 feet (55 meters) long.

LIFE AT SEA

The average crew of a Viking longship was about forty men. They were chosen from volunteers, and had to be strong and skilled in pulling an oar. On short raids, as many warriors would be crammed onto the ship as possible.

Life at sea was crowded, wet and uncomfortable. Because there was so little room, the crew had to follow very strict rules. No quarreling was allowed on board, and women were forbidden to accompany the men on raids. Special regulations decided how the plunder should be divided up. At sea there was always plenty of work to do. When the wind blew and the waves grew high, the crew had to desperately bale out the ship to keep it afloat. In the winter, the spray would turn to ice as it hit the boat, and this had to be chipped away from the sides. In good weather the sailors would busy themselves mending the sails and rigging.

On long voyages, the sailors needed plenty of food. It was very difficult to cook on board, so they took provisions like dried meat, hard-baked bread, smoked fish, apples, cheese, beer and water. To protect themselves from the intense cold of the open sea, the crew wore clothes made from animal skins. At night they rolled themselves up in woolen sleeping bags, and sometimes erected a sort of tent over the ship.

Despite hardships and dangers, the Vikings were able to cross the Atlantic Ocean in their little ships.

Opposite *A longship in rough seas.*

This tenth-century carved stone shows a longship full of Vikings.

NAVIGATION

Viking sailors were great navigators. They were able to voyage thousands of miles without any of the clever electronic instruments that ships' captains have today. Greenland and Iceland were probably first reached by sailors blown off course by high winds. Later sailors followed their directions.

The sailors worked out their position by observing the height of the sun at noon and by the Pole Star at night. They then used written tables to calculate where they were. On cloudy days, they used "sunstones" – special crystals which helped them locate the sun. In 1948, an archeologist working in Greenland found part of a more complicated device called a bearing dial which the Vikings may have used for navigation.

The sailors had no compasses with which to steer their courses. Instead, they pointed their longships in the direction they wanted to go when they left their home shores. Then they relied on experience and guesswork, as well as the stars and their knowledge of the birds, fishes, cloud types, seaweeds and currents of the waters through which they passed.

A gilded wind vane from a Viking longship.

12

WARRIORS AND WEAPONS

A Viking warrior in full battle dress. His battleax had a cutting edge made of specially hardened metal welded to the rest of the blade.

For 300 years, Europe was terrified by the ferocity of Viking warriors. People at the time described them as "terrible wolves" and "stinging hornets." When they leapt from their ships on a raid, some stories tell of them biting their own shields in their frenzy to get at the enemy.

The favorite weapons of the Vikings were swords, spears and battelaxes. Their swords were long and sharpened at both edges, and the hilts were often beautifully decorated. The battleax had a large curved blade and was a fearsome weapon in the hands of a skilled warrior. The Vikings used two types of spear – a light one for throwing, and a heavy one for thrusting. Men and boys spent many hours practicing spear throwing. It is said that in battle, some warriors were able to catch their opponents' spears in midair, and fling them back at the enemy.

To protect himself, the Viking warrior wore a thick leather tunic. If he was rich enough, he might be able to afford a mail shirt. On his head sat a conical iron helmet, which

Right *A Viking's iron sword was made so that it did not shatter on striking an iron helmet or shield.*

sometimes had a vertical iron bar to protect his face. The Vikings did not usually wear helmets with wings or horns, except for ceremonial occasions. Finally, the Viking warrior would carry a small round shield, which was painted and sometimes covered with leather.

TERRIBLE RAIDERS

The sight of a Viking fleet sailing up a river toward your home was a terrifying experience. Often the raiders arrived without warning. They plundered and killed and then vanished out to sea with their booty.

The first raiding parties were usually quite small. Soon larger bands were setting out, and the Vikings began to settle in the lands they attacked. Often they demanded that the local rulers paid them money called *Danegeld*. By the 860s, the Vikings had many permanent bases abroad. Only the courage of King Alfred the Great stopped them from overrunning all of England. As it was, they occupied most of the north and east of the country, which became known as the *Danelaw*.

Generally, it was Vikings from Denmark who attacked England, France and Germany. In France they established a settlement called Normandy (Land of the Northmen). It was descendants of these Vikings

The routes of the Viking raiders

that William the Conqueror led when he invaded England in 1066.

Meanwhile, Norwegian Vikings raided Scotland, Ireland and the Mediterranean, while the Swedes attacked Russia and made their way overland to Constantinople. Indeed, the origin of the name "Russia" probably comes from Swedish Vikings, who were known as the "Rus."

Vikings sack an English monastery.

ACROSS THE ATLANTIC

While some Vikings were attacking Europe, others were sailing the Atlantic and exploring new lands. A Swedish Viking sailor called Gardar Svavarson is thought to have reached Iceland in about A.D. 860, after being blown there by a great storm. Others soon followed him, and by 960 there were about 50,000 people settled on the island. It was a cold, harsh life for the settlers, but they survived. Their descendants still live in Iceland today.

In 982, Erik the Red sailed into the seas west of Iceland. After braving the icebergs and storms of the north Atlantic, he reached another large island. Although it was even icier and more barren than Iceland,

he called it Greenland. This was to encourage settlers to go and live there. Despite the freezing climate, about 3,000 Vikings made Greenland their home.

An Icelander called Bjarni Thordarson was the first Viking to see a new land west of Greenland. Soon afterwards, Leif Eriksson landed at places which they called Helluland (modern Baffin Island), Markland

Viking explorers ventured into the icy waters of Baffin Island, off present-day Canada's north coast.

(Labrador) and Vinland (New-foundland). The old Viking stories tell how Leif and his men spent several years exploring these lands, before attacks by "Skraelings" – native Americans or Inuit – forced them to return to Greenland. In 1962, the remains of a Viking settlement were found in Newfoundland.

Viking routes across the Atlantic took them to Iceland, Greenland and North America.

TRADERS AND MARKETS

Not every Viking sailor set out across the sea in search of plunder and conquest. Many were traders who sailed to distant lands to buy and sell. Others were merchants and craftsmen, who lived in large market towns like Kaupang in Norway, Birka in Sweden and Hedeby in Denmark.

One of the most famous Viking trade routes was southward across

The iron coin die (right) was used for striking the lead trial pieces (top) and the silver Viking coins, which were used in trade.

Russia. Every year, Swedish Vikings set out in their ships laden with cloth, furs, honey and slaves. Once across the Baltic Sea, they sailed their boats along the Russian rivers. When one river became too small or shallow, they dragged the ships overland to join another. After months of travel they eventually reached the Black Sea. They then sailed on to Constantinople, where they exchanged their goods for silks, spices and wines.

In Scandinavia, the greatest trading town in the Viking world was Hedeby. It was known as "the

wonder of the north," for it was full of warehouses, workshops and barns, and its river was crowded with ships. Merchants from all over Europe thronged the streets, bargaining with the local craftsmen. Arabs made the long journey northward to buy slaves, while Vikings from every part of Scandinavia came to buy cloth, jewelery and tools to work their farms and build their ships.

Traders gathered to buy and sell at the Viking town of Hedeby.

FAMILY LIFE

A Viking house usually had only one room, where the family lived and ate.

Most Viking families, including uncles, aunts, cousins and grandparents, as well as parents and children, lived together in longhouses, with walls made from wattle and daub. The roofs often stretched right down to the ground and were covered with turf to keep out the cold. If the weather was very cold, the animals might be brought in, too. Viking houses had little furniture. Benches on which everyone sat and slept ran around the walls.

The family cooked their food on a fire pit in the center of the house. The smoke was supposed to go out through the small hole in the roof, but it often filled the house instead. A normal Viking meal might include thick slices of bread, vegetables and the occasional lump of boiled meat. This would be washed down with buttermilk, or whey. At a feast, the men would drink beer, and a strong drink called mead, made from honey.

Viking children were brought up at home. There were no schools, and very few children learned to write runes – the Viking alphabet. Children were given a name at birth, but Vikings enjoyed giving nicknames. When a child grew older, he might be given one like Keith "Flatnose," or Ragnar "Hairy Breeches." Boys were taught to help with the farmwork. They also learned to ride, swim, hunt, fish and handle weapons. By law, they became adults at 12 years old, and some even sailed on Viking raids at this age.

Girls were expected to help their mothers in the home. They learned how to cook, bake bread, milk cows and make cheese and butter. In the dark, cold winters they would spin and weave woolen cloth for clothes and blankets. Fathers normally chose husbands for their daughters, but it was unusual for a girl to be forced to marry someone she did not like. Girls could also divorce their husbands quite easily if they wished.

An excavated Viking house in the Orkney Islands north of Scotland.

FISHING AND FARMING

A Viking sailor was often a fisherman as well as a farmer. He might spend half of his year fishing from his boat, or raiding abroad, and the other half farming his land. The sailors fished in the fjords or in the sea. They caught cod and haddock in the Atlantic, herring in the Baltic and whales, seals and walruses in the cold, northern seas. They also collected seaweed. They spread it over their fields as manure or gave it to the cattle in winter. When times were bad, the Vikings ate it themselves!

Scandinavia is a mountainous country and farming was very hard work. No wonder Viking raiders were so pleased with the rich farm-land they found in England. Viking farms were quite small, and consisted of a few fields or vegetable patches. In the spring, the farmer and his family would sow their crops of barley and oats. When this was done, the farmer himself might leave to go raiding, and his wife would take charge of the farm. Much of the summer was spent herding the cattle on the rich mountain pastures. The women would also make butter and cheese in preparation for the winter.

In the autumn, many of the animals were killed. The meat was then preserved by salting and pickling. When the snows fell and the winter winds began to blow, there was not much work to do on the farm. Some Vikings spent this time hunting for reindeer, bear and wild boar.

Viking women were often left to look after the farm while their sailor husbands were away raiding or exploring.

CLOTHES AND JEWELERY

The Vikings were a proud people, who liked to look their best. Their clothes were usually stitched at home, from wool and linen cloth made by Viking women. The Vikings loved bright colors, so their clothes were dyed in rich reds, blues, greens and yellows.

Viking men and women loved to dress in bright colors.

Women wore long woolen dresses over linen petticoats. Woolen socks and soft shoes of leather protected their legs and feet. Their hair was usually tied back, and fastened with ribbons or a headscarf. Men dressed in sleeveless jerkins, or long coats over woolen shirts and long cloth trousers. Their legs were protected by shaped leggings, and they wore soft shoes, or sometimes tall, leather

Above *Viking jewelery was often made with the gold and silver stolen from English monasteries. Here are two gold brooches and a gold ring.*

Below *A Viking silver ring and necklace. The pendant is the hammer of Thor, a Viking god.*

boots. In the winter, both men and women wore shaggy cloaks made of sheepskin, and fur hats. Children's clothes were probably very similar to those of their parents.

Both sexes liked to wear brooches, bracelets and rings of silver, gold or bronze. Viking craftsmen decorated these ornaments with beautiful designs. Some of the gold and silver used to make jewelery was part of the plunder Viking raiders stole from European churches and monasteries.

27

GODS AND LEGENDS

The Vikings worshiped many gods. The gods were important to Viking sailors because it was believed they controlled the weather. The Vikings also believed that the gods lived in a great city called Asgard. In this city was a magnificent hall, named Valhalla, where warriors who had died in battle feasted and sported forever.

Odin was the greatest of the Viking gods. He could change his shape into a bird or an animal in a flash, and control winds or tempests with a word. Odin was the father of all the other gods. He was mysterious and dangerous, and everyone feared him.

Thor was a much more popular god. He was not very clever, but he had tremendous strength, and he laughed a lot. Vikings believed he rode across the sky in a chariot pulled by goats, waving his great stone hammer. This caused thunder and lightning. Thursday is named after Thor. This was the day when Vikings held great feasts in his honor.

ODIN **THOR**

FREY

A bronze statue of Thor, with his hammer, found in Iceland.

Frey was the god of love, marriage and all things that grew. He controlled the rain and sunshine. In the autumn, the Vikings carried wooden statues of Frey across their fields. They hoped this would make next year's crops grow well.

The Vikings did not build churches or temples. They held their ceremonies in the open air, where they believed evil spirits could not hinder them. Much of our knowledge about Viking gods and legends comes from stories called sagas. These were told to children by their parents, and written down in Iceland in the 12th and 13th centuries.

Right *This Viking graveyard in Denmark has about 700 graves.*

TWILIGHT OF THE VIKING AGE

By about 1100, the great days of Viking raids and exploration were over. In Scandinavia, the kings of Denmark, Norway and Sweden were uniting their countries and making stronger rules. Vikings could not go raiding whenever they wanted. Soon they were leading a more settled life, content to be farmers and craftsmen.

When important Vikings died, they were sometimes buried at sea.

At the same time, the Vikings became Christians. Denmark was the first country to be converted. Christianity made the Vikings more peaceful, and changed their way of life.

The Vikings were much more than just savage fighters. Their skills as shipbuilders, craftsmen and explorers has become part of our heritage. The Viking sailor, battling against the Atlantic waves in his little ship, deserves our admiration.

GLOSSARY

Adz A carpenter's tool used for chipping.

Archeologist Someone who studies the past from things that earlier people have left behind.

Bale out To empty water from a boat.

Booty Valuables stolen or captured on a raid.

Convert To convince someone of the truth of something.

Crossbeam A large supporting beam stretching from one side of a boat to another.

Divorce The ending of a marriage.

Frenzy To be fighting mad.

Hornet A large stinging insect.

Inuit The people who lived in the Arctic regions of North America and in Greenland. They are also called Eskimos.

Keel The long, heavy piece of wood or metal that forms the base of the framework of a boat and keeps it upright when it is in the water.

Mail Armor made of small iron rings.

Native Americans The only people living in much of North America before Europeans came. They are also called Indians.

Plunder Another word for booty.

Pole Star The star which is nearest in the sky to the North Pole. It is also called the North Star.

Provisions Essential food and supplies taken on a journey.

Rigging The ropes which hold up the mast and work the sails in a sailing ship.

Runes Letters which made up the Viking alphabet.

Spin To twist fibers like wool or cotton into thread.

Volunteer Someone who goes willingly on an expedition or raid.

Warehouse A large building for storing grain or other goods.

Wattle and daub Building material made of sticks covered with clay.

Weave To make cloth from thread.

INDEX

Picture acknowledgments

The pictures in this book were supplied by the following: BPCC/Aldus Archive 27 (both), 29 (top); Sheridan Photo Library 7 (both), 10, 12, 15, 23; The Wayland Picture Library 29 (bottom); The York Archaeological Trust 20.